# Saltwater Fish

Tom Greve

ROURKE PUBLISHING

www.rourkepublishing.com

www.rourkepublishing.com

PHOTO CREDITS: Cover: © Roman Vintonyak; Title Page: © Dirk-jan Mattaar; Page 2, 3: © stephan kerkhofs; Page 4, 5: © Martin Strmko, Piboon Srimak; Page 6: © Richard Carey; Page 7: © Richard Carey, Deborah Coles, Frhojdysz; Page 8: © Ian Scott, Olga N. Vasik; Page 9: © Ian Scott, Cigdem Cooper; Page 10: © Tommy Schultz, Richard Carey, David Pedre; Page 11: © Hotshotsworldwide, Krzysztof Odziomek; Page 12: © Bob Hemphill Broadcast Design; Page 13: © NOAA - David Shale; Page 14: © NOAA, Matt Wilson/Jay Clark, Dirk-jan Mattaar, Sburel; Page 15: © Chris Dascher; Page 16: © Demid; Page 17: © Davidyoung11111; Page 18: © US Coast Guard; Page 19: © Wild Wonders of Europe/Zankl; Page 20: © Doug Perrine; Page 22: © Dirk-jan Mattaar;

Edited by Precious McKenzie

Cover Design by Renee Brady
Interior Design by Tara Raymo

### Library of Congress Cataloging-in-Publication Data

Greve, Tom
 Saltwater Fish / Tom Greve.
     p. cm. -- (Eye to Eye with Animals)
 ISBN 978-1-61741-774-0 (hard cover) (alk. paper)
 ISBN 978-1-61741-976-8 (soft cover)
 Library of Congress Control Number: 2011924819

Rourke Publishing
Printed in the United States of America, North Mankato, Minnesota
060711
060711CL

## ROURKE PUBLISHING

www.rourkepublishing.com - rourke@rourkepublishing.com
Post Office Box 643328  Vero Beach, Florida 32964

# Table of Contents

## Chapter 1

# The Ocean: Earth's Saltwater Mansion

Thousands of the Earth's most **exotic** creatures live in a place where humans wouldn't survive – underwater!

Water covers more than 70 percent of Earth's surface. Almost all of it is saltwater contained in the Earth's oceans.

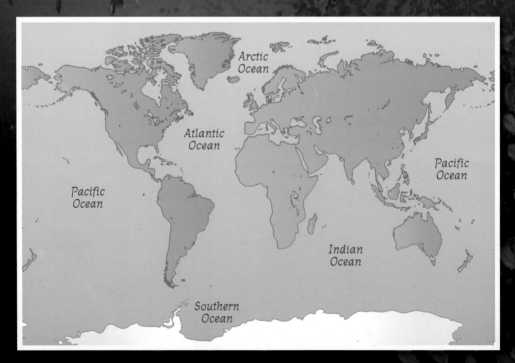

 *Ninety-seven percent of the world's water is saltwater.*

With such a vast **habitat,** it's no wonder saltwater fish are one of Earth's most **diverse,** mysterious, and, in some cases, downright strange group of animals.

◀◀

*Scientists say there are many kinds of saltwater fish that have yet to be discovered.*

Saltwater fish live in an underwater world where activities like breathing, moving, and sleeping are totally different from animals that live on land.

Fish breathe underwater using **gills.** They move underwater by wiggling their bodies and by using their **fins.**

gills

*Black Grouper*

The bodies of most saltwater fish are covered in scales. Their bodies are kept warm or cold by the temperature of the water. ▶▶

Silver Snapper

To help them survey their habitat for **predators,** many fish have eyes that allow them to see up, down, front, and back all at the same time. ▶▶

Grouper

## FREAKY FISH FACT

Since their eyes are kept moist by the water, most fish have no eyelids. They sleep with their eyes open!

Fish can either live in saltwater or freshwater. Saltwater fish **adapt** to life in water that has salt in it, like the ocean. Freshwater fish live in lakes, rivers, or streams where the water is virtually salt-free.

Salmon live in the ocean but swim into riverbeds to lay their eggs. They are one of just a few kinds of fish that can adapt to both salt and fresh water.

*Puffer Fish*

Saltwater fish adapt their behavior and appearance to whichever part of the ocean they live in, and to the dangers they face from predators.

## FREAKY FISH FACT

Puffer Fish have a highly developed method of warding off predators. Not only are they poisonous, they can instantly double in size by sucking in water.

◄◄

*Puffer Fish are also known as Blowfish.*

# Chapter 2

# Fish of All Shapes and Sizes

Scientists put saltwater fish into two main groups.

In one group are fish that have jaws. This group is then divided between fish with bony skeletons, which include most kinds of fish, and fish that have skeletons made of **cartilage**, like sharks and rays.

The second group includes fish without jaws, which include lamprey and hagfish.

▲▲ Tuna have jaws and a bony skeleton.

▲▲ Stingrays have jaws and skeletons made of cartilage.

▲▲ Lampreys are jaw-less fish. Their mouths are designed to suc[k] instead of chew.

The range of sizes among saltwater fish is incredible. In one part of the ocean there are fish that grow to be only a centimeter long, while in another part of the ocean there are fish bigger than a school bus.

SMALLEST!

◀◀ *The tiny dwarf goby fish is smaller than the end of a person's pinky finger.*

BIGGEST!

## FREAKY FISH FACT

Don't let its name fool you. Whale Sharks, like all sharks, are fish. Whales and dolphins, however, are mammals.

*The world's largest fish is the Whale Shark. It can grow to be nearly 60 feet long (18 meters), but it mostly eats tiny sea creatures and small fish.*

Near the ocean's surface, there is sunlight and very little water pressure.

But deep down, the ocean is dark and cold, with crushing pressure from all that water.

Fish living in the deep ocean have made strange adaptations to survive in the harsh habitat.

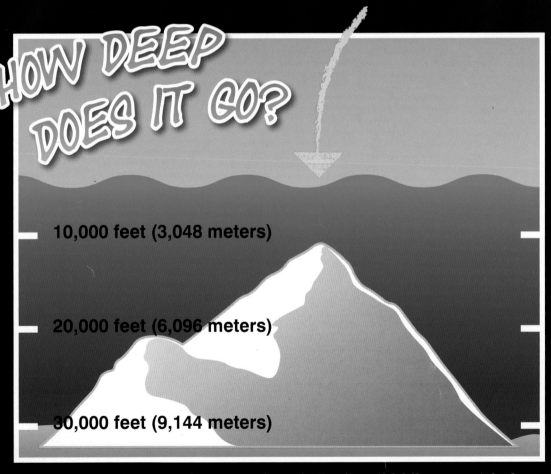

## HOW DEEP DOES IT GO?

10,000 feet (3,048 meters)

20,000 feet (6,096 meters)

30,000 feet (9,144 meters)

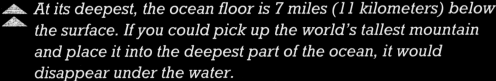

*At its deepest, the ocean floor is 7 miles (11 kilometers) below the surface. If you could pick up the world's tallest mountain and place it into the deepest part of the ocean, it would disappear under the water.*

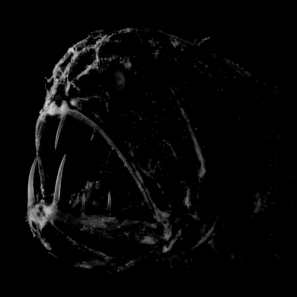

# FREAKY FISH FACT

The fangtooth is among the deepest-living fish ever discovered. They get their name from their huge teeth which are the largest, proportionate to body size, of any fish.

▲ *Looking like a deep-sea monster, fangtooth fish find food near the ocean floor.*

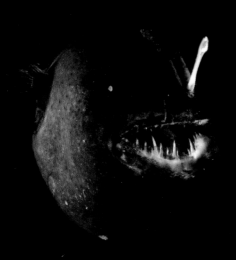

# FREAKY FISH FACT

Female anglerfish use their light to attract **prey.** They eat other sea creatures and fish that come nearby. Females also kill the much smaller males during mating.

▲ *Female anglerfish have a bizarre arm sticking out of their heads that can light up the darkness at the bottom of the ocean.*

## Chapter 3
# Fish Food

Saltwater fish spend their lives as links in a vast but fragile ocean food chain. It starts at the water's surface, where tiny plant organisms called phytoplankton use sunlight and oxygen to survive. Tiny floating animals called zooplankton eat the phytoplankton.

## *An Ocean Food Chain*

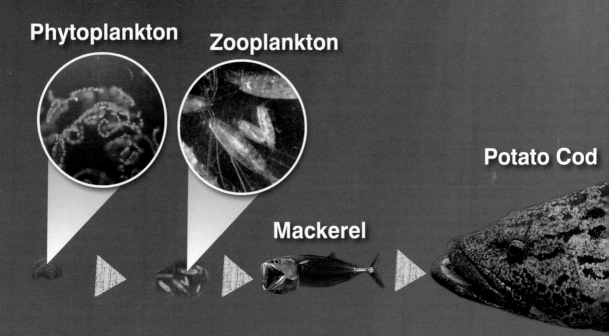

**Phytoplankton**

**Zooplankton**

**Potato Cod**

**Mackerel**

Small fish feed on the zooplankton and larger fish feed on the small fish. When people catch and eat seafood, they impact the ocean's food chain.

# FEARSOME FISH!

The great white shark is the top predator in the ocean. They are capable of killing and eating any living thing they come across. They are also one of the few ocean fish that give birth to live young. Most fish are born from eggs released by the mother.

**Great White Shark**

## Chapter 4

# Threats to the Ocean's Fish

Humans around the world love seafood. But over time, some fish species have become harder and harder to find because of **overfishing.**

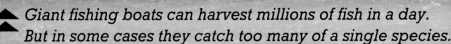

*Giant fishing boats can harvest millions of fish in a day. But in some cases they catch too many of a single species.*

When humans deplete one kind of fish, the predators above that fish in the ocean food chain may die or have to **migrate** because their food source has disappeared.

◀◀

*Overfishing collapsed the population of North Atlantic cod in the early 1990's.*

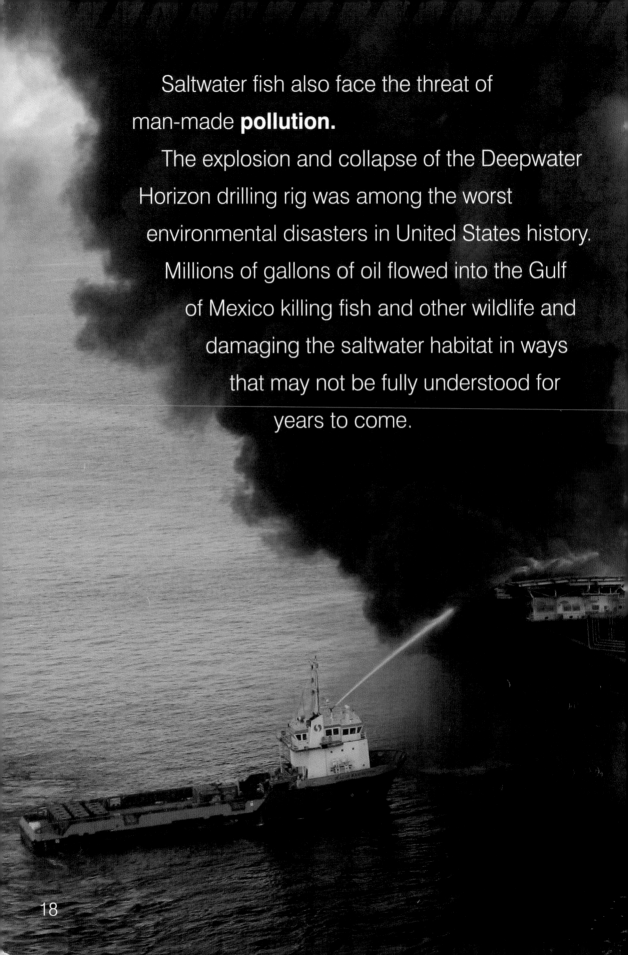

Saltwater fish also face the threat of man-made **pollution.**

The explosion and collapse of the Deepwater Horizon drilling rig was among the worst environmental disasters in United States history. Millions of gallons of oil flowed into the Gulf of Mexico killing fish and other wildlife and damaging the saltwater habitat in ways that may not be fully understood for years to come.

◀◀
*Atlantic bluefin tuna face a double threat. They've already been overfished, and the Gulf oil disaster happened in the same waters where many of them lay their eggs.*

## Chapter 5

# Save the Fish

With some species and their habitats facing man-made threats, ocean **conservation** groups are trying to protect endangered fish, other ocean creatures, and the ocean itself from further damage.

Governments in many **coastal** countries must balance ocean conservation **policy** with the interests of the fishing **industry.**

*Giant nets lost or abandoned by fishing boats float in the ocean and kill millions of fish. They are called ghost nets. Conservation groups work to find and remove them from the water, but it's hard and expensive work.*

North
America

Pacific
Ocean

South
America

⭐ - Marine Sanctuary

The U.S. has set up large ocean sanctuaries where commercial fishing and other human activity is either illegal or highly regulated. Other countries are doing the same.

*Raccoon Butterfly Fish*

While most of their massive ocean habitat remains a mystery to humans, saltwater fish are among the most diverse and adaptable animals on Earth. Overfishing and pollution have harmed some species. With so much ocean to study, scientists continue to unravel the mysteries of saltwater fish and life under the sea.

# Glossary

**adapt** (uh-DAPT): change over time to accommodate a situation

**cartilage** (KAR-tuh-lij): strong, elastic tissue

**coastal** (KOHST-uhl): land next to the ocean

**conservation** (kon-sur-VAY-shuhn): the protection of valuable or rare things

**diverse** (dye-VURSS): varied, assorted

**exotic** (eg-ZOT-ik): strange and fascinating

**fins** (FINZ): body parts of fish that help it move and steer through water

**gills** (GILZ): internal breathing organs of fish

**habitat** (HAB-uh-tat): the place and natural conditions that an animal lives in

**industry** (IN-duh-stree): a single kind of business or trade

**migrate** (MYE-grate): move from one place to another

**overfishing** (OH-vuhr-FISH-ing): catching so many fish of a single species that they become scarce

**policy** (PAH-li-see): a plan by the government to take action

**pollution** (puh-LOO-shuhn): harmful materials that damage or contaminate the environment

**predators** (PRED-uh-turz): animals that hunt other animals for food

**prey** (PRAY): an animal that is hunted by another animal for food

# Index

## Websites To Visit

Nationalgeographic.org

SaveTheSeas.org

WWF.org

Globio.org

OceanConservancy.org

## About the Author

Tom Greve lives in Chicago with his wife Meg and their children Madison and William.  He loves the outdoors, and finds Earth's oceans fascinating.